The Family Kitchen
SLOW COOKING

Contents

Published by Hinkler Books Pty Ltd
45–55 Fairchild Street
Heatherton Victoria 3202 Australia
www.hinkler.com.au

Text and images © Anthony Carroll 2010
Design and layout © Hinkler Books Pty Ltd 2013
Page layout: Dynamo Limited
Prepress: Splitting Image

ISBN: 978 1 7430 8340 6

Printed and bound in China

Introduction

Having a slow cooker is like having a genie at home, cooking while you're away. When you get back, dinner awaits, without fear of it drying out or overcooking. The slow cooker is also a marvellous food warmer and server. It's ideal for heat-and-serve dishes and excellent for buffets or family dinners.

Here are some hints and tips for making the best use of your slow cooker:

- Slow cookers are economical to run and make good use of cheaper cuts of meat, such as casserole steak and neck of lamb. The long, slow cooking time is also perfect for dried pulses.

- It's best to brown meat in a frying pan or in the oven prior to placing it into the slow cooker. This will enhance the flavour and appearance of your dish. You will get an even better result if you deglaze the frying pan or roasting dish with a little stock or wine, then add this to your cooker.

- You will find that cooking times vary considerably, even when cooking the same recipe a second time. Timing depends very much on the tenderness and texture of the particular food being cooked.

- Avoid lifting the lid during cooking if possible, because this will lead to loss of heat and increase the cooking time. The lid also helps to retain moisture and flavour.

- Don't put frozen or very cold foods in the slow cooker if the appliance has been pre-heated or is hot to the touch.

- Extreme caution must be used when moving the appliance containing hot oil or other liquids.

- Always attach the cord to the appliance first, then plug it into the wall outlet. To disconnect, turn any control to off, then remove the plug.

Soups

The slow cooker's wrap-around heating method is perfect for soups. There is no risk of the food sticking or scorching on the bottom of the pan so there is no need to keep stirring as it cooks.

Minestrone

Serves 6–8 · Preparation and cooking 10 hours 25 minutes

1 veal shank, trimmed of fat

1 clove garlic, crushed

1 medium carrot, finely chopped

1 large onion, chopped

2 cups beef stock (broth)

1 teaspoon salt

1 teaspoon freshly ground black pepper

3 cups tomato juice

3 tomatoes, chopped

2 teaspoons yeast extract

2 bay leaves

1 sprig thyme

½ cup parsley, chopped

½ cup macaroni

60g (2oz) cabbage, shredded

parmesan cheese, grated, to garnish

1 Combine all ingredients (except cheese) in the slow cooker. Simmer for at least 10 hours on low.

2 Remove shank from soup once meat is falling from bone, and chop meat coarsely. Replace meat in slow cooker and cook on high until thoroughly reheated.

3 Taste the soup, and if the tomatoes have made it 'sharp', add a little raw sugar. Garnish with parmesan cheese and serve with crusty bread.

Creamy Pumpkin Soup

Serves 6–8 · Preparation and cooking 4½–6½ hours

500g (1lb) bright yellow pumpkin, peeled and cut into chunks

2 cups tomato juice

1 tablespoon raw sugar

2 chicken stock cubes (bouillon), crumbled

dash of hot chilli (pepper) sauce

1 bay leaf

salt and freshly ground black pepper

½ cup thickened (whipping) cream

¼ cup parsley, chopped

1 Combine all ingredients except cream and parsley in slow cooker with 8 cups of water. Cook until pumpkin is tender, approximately 4–5 hours on low or 3 hours on high.

2 Remove bay leaf and process the mixture, a cupful at a time, in a blender or food processor. Return mixture to slow cooker and reheat. About 1 hour before serving, add cream and allow to heat through. Serve sprinkled with fresh parsley.

Tomato, Lentil and Basil Soup

Serves 4 · Preparation and cooking 3 hours 40 minutes

½ cup brown lentils

1kg (2lb) Roma tomatoes

2 onions, diced

2 tablespoons tomato paste (purée)

3 cups vegetable stock (broth)

1 bay leaf

freshly ground black pepper

½ cup fresh basil, chopped, plus extra leaves for garnish

1 Rinse the lentils, drain and add them to a large saucepan of boiling water. Simmer, covered, for 25 minutes or until tender, then drain, rinse and set aside.

2 Meanwhile, place the tomatoes in a bowl, cover with boiling water and leave for 30 seconds, then drain. Remove the skins, deseed and chop.

3 In a slow cooker on high, add the onions and stir in the tomatoes, tomato paste (purée), stock (broth), bay leaf and pepper. Cover and simmer for 2¼ hours.

4 Remove and discard the bay leaf, then purée the soup until smooth in a food processor or with a hand-held blender. Stir in the lentils and chopped basil, then reheat on high. Serve garnished with the fresh basil leaves.

Roasted Red Vegetable and Bread Soup

Serves 4 · Preparation and cooking 4 hours

2 tablespoons olive oil

1kg (2lb) Roma tomatoes

2 red capsicums (peppers)

3 cloves garlic, crushed

2 onions, finely diced

2 teaspoons ground cumin

1 teaspoon ground coriander

4 cups chicken stock (broth)

2 slices white bread, crusts removed and torn into pieces

1 tablespoon balsamic vinegar

salt and freshly ground black pepper

1 Preheat oven to 180°C (160°C fan, 350°F, gas 4). Lightly oil a baking dish, place tomatoes and capsicums (peppers) in the dish and bake for 20 minutes or until the skins have blistered. Add in the garlic, onion, cumin and coriander for the last 5 minutes. Set aside to cool, then take out the tomatoes and capsicums, remove their skins and roughly chop.

2 Set slow cooker on high, add the cooked vegetables and stock (broth) and cook for 2 hours. Add bread, balsamic vinegar and salt and pepper, and cook for a further 50 minutes.

Pea and Ham Soup

Serves 6–8 · Preparation and cooking 8½–12 hours

1½ cups yellow or green dried peas

1 onion, diced

2 bay leaves

1 sprig thyme

salt and freshly ground black pepper

1 medium smoked ham hock

8 cups chicken or vegetable stock (broth)

1   Rinse peas and place in slow cooker. Add all remaining ingredients to slow cooker and cook on low for at least 8 hours. This soup improves with long, slow cooking, so 10–12 hours will enhance the flavour.

2   Remove bay leaves, thyme and ham hock. Cut the fat off the hock, chop the meat and replace it in the soup. Serve very hot.

Scallop Chowder

Serves 4–6 · Preparation and cooking 2½–3 hours

12 scallops, diced

½ cup white wine

1 sprig thyme

1 bay leaf

1 cup thickened (whipping) cream

12 cups milk

2 cups chicken stock (broth)

salt and freshly ground black pepper

6 spring (green) onions, chopped

1 Place scallops into slow cooker with white wine and herbs and cook on low for 1 hour.

2 Combine remaining ingredients and add to slow cooker. Cook on high for 1–1½ hours or on low for 1½–2 hours until heated through, but do not overcook.

Meat

Slow cooking, made possible by low temperatures, is the key to fine flavour, juiciness and lack of shrinkage, especially with meat. Try these recipes for tasty, melt-in-the-mouth main courses.

Beef and Vegetable Casserole

Serves 4 · Preparation and cooking 4½–8½ hours

500g (1lb) blade steak, trimmed and cubed

2 white onions, thinly sliced

425g (15oz) canned Roma tomatoes

1 beef stock cube (bouillon), crumbled

½ clove garlic, crushed

½ teaspoon dried marjoram

¼ cup parsley, chopped

salt and freshly ground black pepper

250g (8oz) zucchini (courgette), sliced

1 Place beef and onion in slow cooker. Add the tomatoes, reserving ¼ cup juice, mix the stock cube (bouillon) into the juice, then add to cooker with the garlic, marjoram and half the parsley. Season to taste.

2 Cook on low for 6–8 hours or on high for 4–5 hours. About 1 hour before serving, add the zucchini (courgette) and stir through half the remaining parsley. Serve sprinkled with the last of the parsley.

Beef Pie

Serves 6 · Preparation and cooking 7½–9½ hours

2 tablespoons vegetable oil

1kg (2lb) blade or topside steak, cubed

1 onion, chopped

2 tablespoons plain (all-purpose) flour

2 beef stock cubes (bouillon), crumbled

1 teaspoon of yeast extract

1 tablespoon tomato paste (purée)

½ teaspoon salt

¼ cup parsley, chopped

1 teaspoon Worcestershire sauce

hot chilli (pepper) sauce

250g (8oz) pre-made puff pastry

2 tablespoons milk

1 Heat oil in frying pan (skillet) and brown the beef and onion, then transfer to slow cooker using a slotted spoon. Add the flour to the juices in the pan, brown it, and pour in 1 cup water. Add the stock cubes (bouillon), yeast extract, tomato paste (purée) and salt, and bring to the boil, stirring.

2 Pour liquid into slow cooker with the parsley, Worcestershire sauce and chilli (pepper) sauce to taste, and cook on low for at least 6–8 hours or overnight. Test meat for tenderness, then spoon beef mixture into a greased pie dish and allow to cool.

3 Preheat the oven to 190ºC (170ºC fan, 375ºF, gas 5). Slice puff pastry into long strips. Brush rim of pie dish with a little milk and fit a pastry strip around the wet rim, then use remaining strips to create a lattice across the meat. Brush lightly with milk and bake pie for 25–30 minutes.

Spaghetti and Meatballs

Serves 4 · Preparation and cooking 4 hours 25 minutes

500g (1lb) minced (ground) beef

2 white onions, finely chopped

1 clove garlic, crushed

1 tablespoon vegetable oil

½ teaspoon dried basil

1 bay leaf

salt and freshly ground black pepper

400g (14oz) canned tomatoes, drained

2 teaspoons Worcestershire sauce

3 tablespoons tomato paste (purée)

500g (1lb) wholemeal spaghetti

30g (1oz) parmesan cheese, grated

1 Mix together meat, onion and garlic, and roll into small balls. Heat the oil in a frying pan (skillet), add the meatballs and sauté until lightly browned.

2 Place meatballs into slow cooker and add all remaining ingredients, except pasta and cheese. Cook on low for approximately 4 hours.

3 Bring a large saucepan of salted water to the boil, add the spaghetti and cook for 8 minutes or until just firm in the centre (al dente). Drain, then add to slow cooker and stir through sauce. Serve sprinkled with parmesan cheese.

Chilli Beef Tacos

Serves 6 · Preparation and cooking 4½–5½ hours

2 teaspoons vegetable oil

500g (1lb) minced (ground) beef

2 onions, chopped

60g (2oz) taco seasoning mix

½ teaspoon freshly ground black pepper

2 tablespoons tomato paste (purée)

½ cup beef stock (broth)

6 taco shells or corn tortillas

To serve

tomatoes

cucumber

lettuce

cheese

1 Heat the oil in a frying pan (skillet), and sauté the beef until browned. Add onion and cook until slightly softened. Stir in taco mix, pepper and tomato paste (purée) and cook for 1–2 minutes. Add stock (broth) and stir.

2 Transfer mixture to slow cooker and cook for approximately 4 hours on low. If mixture is too wet at the end of the cooking time, remove the cooker lid and cook on high until liquid has reduced.

3 Spoon beef mixture into heated taco shells or tortillas and serve at once with bowls of chopped tomatoes, cucumber, lettuce and cheese.

Lamb Shanks with Orange

Serves 4 · Preparation and cooking 8½–10½ hours

4 lamb shanks, trimmed of fat

2 white onions, sliced

3 oranges, sliced

1 lemon, sliced

1 cup dry white wine

½ cup chicken stock (broth)

salt and freshly ground black pepper

2 bay leaves or 1 sprig rosemary

1 tablespoon Grand Marnier

1 Place shanks in slow cooker and arrange onions, oranges and lemon between and around shanks.

2 Mix wine and stock (broth) and season to taste. Place bay leaves or rosemary sprig on shanks and pour over wine mixture. Cook on low for approximately 8 hours or overnight.

3 To serve, remove cooked citrus slices and bay leaves and skim off as much surface fat as possible. Remove shanks carefully and place on a heated serving platter, then add liqueur to liquid, heat through on high and pour over shanks. Garnish with extra half-slices of orange and fresh herbs.

Lancashire Hotpot

Serves 4–6 · Preparation and cooking 8½–10½ hours

8 neck or chump lamb chops, trimmed of fat

6 carrots, peeled and thinly sliced

6 parsnips, peeled and thinly sliced

6 onions, peeled and thinly sliced

6 potatoes, peeled, parboiled and sliced

salt and freshly ground black pepper

¼ cup parsley, chopped

1 Layer all ingredients except parsley in the slow cooker, ending with a layer of potatoes. Cover with water and cook on low for 8 hours or overnight, until lamb is falling off bones. Skim off any fat.

2 To serve, ladle out the meat and vegetables, spoon over the flavoursome juices and sprinkle with parsley.

Greek Lamb with Rosemary

Serves 6 · Preparation and cooking 5½–8½ hours

1.5kg (3lb) lamb, trimmed and cubed

1 large white onion, finely sliced

2 teaspoons dried rosemary

¼ teaspoon freshly ground black pepper

¼ teaspoon salt

1 cup chicken or veal stock (broth)

¼ cup dry white wine

1 tablespoon plain (all-purpose) flour

3 rosemary sprigs

1 Place lamb in slow cooker with all other ingredients except rosemary sprigs. Cook on low for approximately 6–8 hours or on high for approximately 5–6 hours.

2 If a thicker gravy is preferred, mix together some of the cooking liquid with plain (all-purpose) flour. Either pour mixture back into slow cooker and cook on high until thickened, stirring occasionally, or gently heat flour mixture on the stovetop in a small saucepan, whisking until thickened, before pouring back into the slow cooker.

3 Garnish with rosemary sprigs and serve.

Lamb and Spinach Curry

Serves 4 · Preparation and cooking 7½ hours

2 tablespoons vegetable oil

2 onions, chopped

2 cloves garlic, chopped

25mm (1in) piece fresh ginger (gingerroot), finely chopped

1 cinnamon stick

¼ teaspoon ground cloves

3 cardamom pods

750g (1½lb) lamb, diced

1 tablespoon ground cumin

1 tablespoon ground coriander

⅓ cup natural yoghurt

2 tablespoons tomato paste (purée)

¾ cup beef stock (broth)

salt and freshly ground black pepper

120g (4oz) baby spinach, chopped

2 tablespoons blanched almonds, toasted

1 Heat the oil in a large heavy-based saucepan. Add onions, garlic, ginger (gingerroot), cinnamon, cloves and cardamom and cook for 5 minutes. Add the lamb and cook for 5 minutes, turning, until it begins to brown.

2 Transfer mixture to slow cooker set on high. Mix in the cumin and coriander, then add the yoghurt 1 tablespoon at a time, stirring well each time. Mix the tomato paste (purée) and stock (broth) together and add to the cooker. Season to taste, then reduce the heat to low and cook for 7 hours.

3 Stir in the spinach, cover and simmer for another 15 minutes or until the mixture has reduced slightly. Remove the cinnamon stick and the cardamom pods and mix in the almonds. Serve with rice.

Slow-cooked Lamb Roast

Serves 4 · Preparation and cooking 3½–8½ hours

1.5kg (3lb) lamb roast

2 cloves garlic, cut into slivers

bunch fresh rosemary

2 tablespoons olive oil

30g (1oz) butter

1 large onion, sliced

400g (14oz) canned butter beans, drained and rinsed

¼ cup flat-leaf parsley, chopped

½ cup chicken stock (broth)

salt and freshly ground black pepper

1 Make small incisions all over lamb with a very sharp knife, then stuff each with a sliver of garlic and a sprig of rosemary.

2 Heat oil in a large frying pan (skillet), cook lamb until browned all over. Remove from pan and transfer to slow cooker.

3 In the same pan, add butter and cook onion for 1–2 minutes or until transparent, then place in slow cooker with remaining ingredients except seasoning.

4 Cover and cook on high for 3–4 hours, or on low for 6–8 hours. Season with salt and pepper.

5 Remove meat from slow cooker and rest for 10 minutes before carving. Serve slices of lamb with beans and parsley sauce.

Poultry

Come home to the delicious aroma of a lemony chicken casserole, a fragrant curry or a tasty fricassée. Whatever the dish, chicken or duck gently braised in a slow cooker will always be tender and succulent.

Mustard Chicken

Serves 3–4 · Preparation and cooking 5½–6½ hours

3 carrots, peeled and diced

3 large onions, finely chopped

1 clove garlic, crushed

2 teaspoons dried thyme

1 bay leaf

salt and seasoned pepper blend

500g (1lb) lean pork, skinned and sliced

1.5kg (3lb) chicken, jointed

4 rashers bacon, rinds removed

½ cup dry white wine

¼ cup brandy

Mustard sauce

1 egg yolk

3 tablespoons thickened (whipping) cream

1 tablespoon Dijon mustard

1. In a bowl, combine the carrot, onion, garlic, herbs and salt and pepper. Place half the pork in the base of the slow cooker, then add half the vegetable mixture. Add the chicken pieces, the remaining vegetable mixture, then the remaining pork. Place bacon rashers on top.

2. Pour over combined wine and brandy. Place a piece of foil over the slow cooker, then cover with lid and cook on low for around 5 hours (cooking time may vary depending on the tenderness of the chicken).

3. To make the sauce, drain off the cooking liquid, skim off any fat and pour into a small saucepan. Beat egg yolk and cream together, add to saucepan and whisk. Cook gently until thick, but do not allow to boil. Add the mustard and whisk until thoroughly blended.

4. Arrange chicken pieces, pork and vegetables on warmed serving platter, and pour over the mustard sauce. Serve with potatoes, sprinkled with parsley.

Moroccan-style Chicken Wings

Serves 6 · Preparation and cooking 9 hours 40 minutes

2 tablespoons vegetable oil

1kg (2lb) chicken wings

1 large onion, finely chopped

1 clove garlic, crushed

2cm (¾in) piece ginger (gingerroot), grated

½ teaspoon ground turmeric

½ teaspoon ground cumin

1 cinnamon stick

¼ cup cider vinegar

2 cups apricot nectar

salt and freshly ground black pepper

90g (3oz) pitted prunes, pitted

90g (3oz) dried apricots

1 tablespoon honey

¼ cup lemon juice

steamed couscous, to serve

1. Heat the oil in a large saucepan and brown the chicken wings in batches. Remove browned wings to a plate. Add the onion to the pan and cook for 2 minutes. Stir in the garlic and cook for a further minute.

2. Transfer the onion and garlic to the slow cooker. Add the chicken, ginger (gingerroot) and spices, and stir to coat wings with spices. Add the vinegar and apricot nectar, season to taste and cook on low for 6 hours.

3. Add the prunes, apricots, honey and lemon juice to the cooker and simmer for 2 more hours. Remove lid, turn to high and simmer for 35 minutes. If a thicker sauce is desired, remove the wings and fruit to a serving platter and simmer until the sauce reduces and thickens. Serve wings immediately on a bed of steamed couscous and pour over the sauce. Garnish with parsley.

Citrus Chicken

Serves 4–5 · Preparation and cooking 4½–6½ hours

1 lemon

1.5kg (3lb) roasting chicken, whole

1 bouquet garni

3 carrots, thinly sliced

6 onions, thinly sliced

½ cup chicken stock (broth)

salt and freshly ground black pepper

pinch of nutmeg (mace)

Cream sauce

170g (6oz) button mushrooms, sliced

½ cup unthickened (half and half) cream

1 Halve the lemon, squeeze out the juice and brush it all over the chicken. Place lemon skins in the chicken cavity.

2 Lightly grease the slow cooker and add the bouquet garni. Place the chicken on top and arrange the carrot and onion around the outside. Pour in the stock (broth), season to taste, add nutmeg (mace), then cook for approximately 6 hours on low or 4–5 hours on high (cooking time will vary depending on the tenderness of the chicken).

3 To make the sauce, sauté the mushrooms. Remove about ½ cup of chicken stock from the slow cooker, skim off as much fat as possible, and bring to the boil in a small saucepan. Add the stock to the mushrooms and reduce, then add the cream and reduce to make a pouring sauce. Serve chicken with the cream sauce.

Nice'n'easy Chinese Chicken

Serves 4 · Preparation and cooking 3½–5 hours

1 tablespoon vegetable oil

4 chicken pieces

2 chicken stock cubes (bouillon), crumbled

1 tablespoon cornflour (cornstarch)

2–3 tablespoons soy sauce

freshly ground black pepper

750g (1½lb) chopped Chinese vegetables (such as bok choy, choy sum and gai lan)

3 spring (green) onions, sliced diagonally

fresh coriander (cilantro), chopped, to garnish

1 Heat the oil in a frying pan (skillet). Remove the skin from the chicken pieces, add to the pan and brown lightly.

2 Transfer chicken to slow cooker and add the stock cubes (bouillon) and ½ cup water. Cook on low for 3–4 hours or on high for approximately 2½–3½ hours (cooking time will vary depending on the tenderness of the chicken).

3 Blend the cornflour (cornstarch) with 1 tablespoon water and pour back into slow cooker, stirring thoroughly. Add soy sauce and pepper.

4 Turn the slow cooker to high, add the Chinese vegetables and cook for approximately 30 minutes. Add spring (green) onions about 15 minutes before the end. Serve with cooked rice or noodles, and sprinkle with chopped coriander (cilantro).

Green Chicken Curry with Lemongrass Rice

Serves 6 · Preparation and cooking 3–4 hours

2 cups coconut milk

1 cup chicken stock (broth)

2 tablespoons green curry paste (jerk seasoning)

3 kaffir lime leaves, shredded

200g (7oz) pumpkin, chopped

4 chicken breast fillets, cubed

120g (4oz) canned bamboo shoots, drained

120g (4oz) snake beans or green (string) beans, chopped

200g (7oz) bok choy, chopped

1 tablespoon fish sauce

1 tablespoon grated palm sugar

¼ cup fresh Thai basil leaves, torn

Lemongrass rice

1½ cups jasmine rice

2 stalks lemongrass, bruised

1 Combine coconut milk, stock (broth), curry paste (jerk seasoning) and lime leaves in a slow cooker on high. Cook until the sauce begins to thicken. Add the pumpkin and cook for 20 minutes or until it starts to soften.

2 Add the chicken and bamboo shoots and cook for 1 hour. Add the beans, bok choy, fish sauce and palm sugar and cook until the vegetables are tender, approximately 1 more hour. Stir through the basil leaves.

3 To make the lemongrass rice, put the rice, lemongrass and 4 cups water in a saucepan. Bring to the boil and cook over a high heat until steam holes appear in the top of the rice. Reduce the heat to low, cover and cook for 10 minutes or until all the liquid is absorbed and the rice is tender. Remove the lemongrass. Serve curry spooned over bowls of rice.

Fricasséed Chicken with Vinegar

Serves 4 · Preparation and cooking 2–2½ hours

¼ cup olive oil

1kg (2lb) chicken thigh fillets, quartered

freshly ground black pepper

2 large cloves garlic, chopped

2 sprigs fresh rosemary, leaves removed and chopped

5 anchovy fillets, chopped

½ cup white wine vinegar

2 tablespoons balsamic vinegar

20 Kalamata olives

1 In a heavy-based frying pan (skillet), heat the olive oil and brown the chicken pieces all over, seasoning well with pepper. Transfer to a plate and keep warm. Turn the heat to low and add garlic, rosemary and anchovies. Stir until the mixture is aromatic.

2 Transfer the garlic mixture and chicken to the slow cooker. Add the white wine vinegar and cook on high for about 1½ hours or until the chicken is tender. Just before serving, stir in the balsamic vinegar and olives.

Duck Braised in Brandy and Port

Serves 4 · Preparation and cooking 5½–6 hours

1kg (2lb) plump duck

4 tablespoons plain (all-purpose) flour

60g (2oz) butter

2 tablespoons olive oil

2 rashers bacon, chopped

1 large onion, chopped

60g (2oz) small mushrooms, sliced

4 tablespoons brandy

4 tablespoons port

salt and freshly ground black pepper

½ teaspoon dried thyme

1 Pat duck dry with absorbent paper and rub lightly with 2 tablespoons flour.

2 Heat butter and oil in a frying pan (skillet) and brown duck on all sides. Remove and place in slow cooker.

3 Add a little extra butter to frying pan if necessary, then add bacon, onion and mushrooms. Sauté until golden brown. Pour half the brandy and half the port into the pan and simmer for 1–2 minutes. Add remaining flour and cook until very well browned.

4 Gradually add 1 cup water, stirring constantly. Season to taste, add thyme and spoon sauce over duck in slow cooker. Cook for approximately 5 hours on low. About 30 minutes before serving, stir remaining port and brandy into sauce around duck. Serve with green vegetables.

Seafood and Vegetarian

A slow cooker preserves the subtle flavour of seafood and is perfect for poaching fish. It is also ideal for steaming delicate dishes such as Spinach Custards, as well as cooking more robust root vegetables and beans.

Citrus and Tarragon Fish

Serves 4 · Preparation and cooking 1½–3 hours

2 teaspoons butter

600g (21oz) white fish fillets

salt and freshly ground black pepper

8 large sprigs tarragon

2 oranges, each cut into four slices

2 lemons, each cut into four slices

4 tablespoons dry white wine

1 Cut four pieces of aluminium foil and lightly butter each. Place a piece of fish on each foil sheet and season to taste.

2 Lay a tarragon sprig on each piece of fish then a slice of orange and a slice of lemon side by side. Turn up the sides of the foil and spoon 1 tablespoon wine over each fish piece, then fold over the foil and seal the parcels. Place in the slow cooker and cook on high for 1–1½ hours or on low for 2–2½ hours.

3 To serve, place parcels on serving plates, open the top of each parcel and replace the cooked herb sprigs and citrus slices with fresh herb sprigs and citrus slices. Alternatively, carefully transfer the fish to the plate, replace the herbs and citrus slices, and spoon the juices over the top.

Smoked Cod Casserole

Serves 6–8 · Preparation and cooking 2 hours 25 minutes

1kg (2lb) smoked cod

1 white onion, sliced

1 cup dry white wine

1 teaspoon peppercorns

1 teaspoon crushed garlic

¼ cup fennel, dill (dill weed) or aniseed, chopped

5 large tomatoes, plus 1 extra, quartered

10 black (ripe) olives, pitted

6 spring (green) onions, chopped into 5cm (2in) lengths

1 Cut fish into serving-size pieces and place with onion, wine, peppercorns, garlic and fennel, dill (dill weed) or aniseed in the slow cooker. Cook on low for approximately 2 hours. Check fish at the end of 1½ hours, as cooking time may vary depending on the tenderness of the fish and whether it has been frozen.

2 During the last 30 minutes of cooking, add four of the tomatoes and the olives. To serve, pour fish and juices into a casserole dish. Fold through the spring (green) onions and garnish with remaining tomato quarters.

Curried Scallops

Serves 6 · Preparation and cooking 2 hours 25 minutes

250g (8oz) scallops

½ cup dry white wine

1 bouquet garni

120g (4oz) butter

1¼ cups unthickened (half and half) cream

½ teaspoon curry powder (jerk seasoning)

salt and freshly ground black pepper

2 egg yolks

2 tablespoons milk

1 Place scallops, white wine and bouquet garni in the slow cooker and cook on low for approximately 1 hour. Pour off and reserve liquid, discard bouquet garni and keep scallops warm in slow cooker.

2 Put cooking liquid with butter into a small saucepan and boil hard to reduce. Stir in the cream, curry powder (jerk seasoning) and salt and pepper, and again boil hard for 2–3 minutes. Remove from heat and allow to cool.

3 Beat egg yolks with milk, and carefully stir into cooled cream mixture. Pour mixture back into slow cooker with the scallops and cook on high for 45–60 minutes. To serve, place a little cooked rice in a small bowl and spoon over 3–4 scallops with a generous quantity of sauce. Serve immediately.

Slow Paella

Serves 8 · Preparation and cooking 2 hours 45 minutes

1 tablespoon olive oil

2 onions, chopped

2 cloves garlic, crushed

4 sprigs fresh thyme, leaves removed and stalks discarded

zest of 1 lemon, finely grated

4 ripe tomatoes, chopped

2½ cups short-grain white rice

pinch of saffron threads, soaked in 2 cups water

5 cups chicken or fish stock (broth), warmed

290g (10oz) peas

2 red capsicums (peppers), chopped

1kg (2lb) mussels, scrubbed and debearded

500g (1lb) firm white fish fillets, chopped

290g (10oz) raw prawns (shrimps), shelled

250g (8oz) scallops

3 calamari, cleaned and sliced

¼ cup parsley, chopped

1 Preheat slow cooker on high. Add the oil and the onion and stir, then add the garlic, thyme, lemon zest and tomatoes and cook for 15 minutes.

2 Add the rice and saffron mixture and warmed stock (broth). Simmer, stirring occasionally, for 1½ hours or until the rice has absorbed almost all the liquid.

3 Stir in the peas, capsicums (peppers) and mussels and cook for 20 minutes. Add the fish, prawns (shrimps) and scallops and cook for 20 minutes. Stir in the calamari and parsley and cook for 20 minutes longer or until the seafood is cooked.

Herbed Cannelloni with Tomato Sauce

Serves 3–4 · Preparation and cooking 2–3 hours

8 instant cannelloni tubes

250g (8oz) cottage cheese

30g (1oz) parmesan cheese, grated

1 teaspoon mixed dried herbs

6 spring (green) onions, finely chopped

salt and freshly ground black pepper

few drops Angostura bitters (optional)

parmesan cheese, shaved, to serve

parsley sprigs, to serve

Tomato sauce

1 cup puréed tomatoes (passata)

3–4 spring (green) onions, chopped

2 teaspoons Worcestershire sauce

4 drops Angostura bitters

1 large clove garlic, crushed

1 Bring a large saucepan of salted water to the boil, add the pasta tubes and cook for 8 minutes or until just firm in the centre (al dente). Drain, set aside and keep warm. Place the cheese, herbs, onions, salt, pepper and bitters in a bowl and mix thoroughly.

2 To make the sauce, mix together all ingredients.

3 Lightly butter the base of the slow cooker. Spoon cheese mixture into cannelloni tubes. Spoon a little tomato sauce into the cooker, then arrange the stuffed cannelloni tubes in the cooker and spoon over remainder of sauce. Cook for 1–1½ hours on high or 2–2½ hours on low. Serve sprinkled with extra parmesan cheese and parsley sprigs.

Spinach Custards

Serves 6–8 · Preparation and cooking 2–3 hours

250g (8oz) cooked spinach or silverbeet, stems removed

120g (4oz) cream cheese

2 small eggs

½ cup milk

1 small onion, peeled and chopped

¼ teaspoon salt

freshly ground black pepper

½ teaspoon dried basil

30g (1oz) parmesan cheese, grated, plus extra to garnish

8 fresh basil sprigs

1 Drain spinach or silverbeet until as dry as possible, then process in a food processor or blender until finely chopped. Add remaining ingredients and half the basil and blend until very smooth.

2 Pour mixture into 6–8 small, buttered ovenproof dishes and cover each with aluminium foil. Place dishes in the slow cooker and pour a little water into base, then cook on high for approximately 1½ hours or on low for 2½ hours.

3 To serve, sprinkle with extra grated cheese and garnish with a basil sprig.

Stuffed Vine Leaves in Tomato Sauce

Serves 4 · Preparation and cooking 2–3 hours

12 grapevine leaves, canned or fresh

olive oil

2 cups cooked brown rice

1 teaspoon dried mixed herbs

pinch of nutmeg (mace)

salt and freshly ground black pepper

1 teaspoon dried garlic or garlic flakes

2 tomatoes, chopped and peeled

¼ cup parsley, chopped

½ teaspoon Angostura bitters (optional)

2 spring (green) onions, chopped finely

Tomato sauce

15g (½oz) butter

1 onion, diced

400g (14oz) canned Roma tomatoes, drained and chopped

2 teaspoons brown sugar

pinch of dried herbs

1 tablespoon tomato paste (purée)

3 tablespoons dry red wine

¼ cup parsley, chopped

1 If you are using fresh vine leaves, remove the stems, pour boiling water over leaves and leave for 1–2 minutes until softened. Dry and lightly wipe each leaf with a drop of oil.

2 Combine all other ingredients to make the filling. Squeeze a handful of filling to make it firm and place onto leaf, then fold into neat little parcel, sealing with a little squeeze. Repeat with remaining leaves. Arrange carefully in base of slow cooker.

3 To make the tomato sauce, heat the butter in a frying pan (skillet) and cook the onion until golden brown. Add all other ingredients and cook until blended. Spoon sauce into slow cooker over vine leaf parcels and cook on high for approximately 1½ hours or on low for 2–2½ hours.

Argentinian Bean
and Vegetable Stew

Serves 4 · Preparation and cooking 2½–3 hours

1 tablespoon olive oil

1 onion, finely diced

2 cloves garlic, crushed

1 red capsicum (pepper), diced

1 jalapeño chilli, deseeded and diced

1 teaspoon sweet paprika

400g (14oz) canned diced tomatoes

2 cups vegetable stock (broth)

250g (8oz) baby (new) potatoes, quartered

250g (8oz) sweet potato (yam), diced

1 carrot, sliced

400g (14oz) canned cannellini (white kidney) beans, rinsed and drained

200g (7oz) Savoy cabbage, shredded

¼ cup fresh coriander (cilantro), chopped

salt and freshly ground black pepper

1 Heat oil in a large frying pan (skillet) over medium heat. Cook onion, garlic, capsicum (pepper) and chilli until soft. Add sweet paprika and cook until aromatic.

2 Transfer contents of frying pan to a slow cooker set on high and add tomatoes and vegetable stock (broth). Stir to combine, then add potatoes, sweet potato (yam) and carrot. Bring to the boil. Reduce heat to low, cover, and simmer for 1½ hours until vegetables are tender.

3 Add beans, cabbage and coriander (cilantro) and season with salt and pepper. Simmer for a further 30 minutes or until cabbage is cooked.

Moroccan Root Vegetable Curry

Serves 4 · Preparation and cooking 4 hours

1 tablespoon olive oil

1 onion, chopped

1 green chilli, deseeded and chopped

1 clove garlic, finely chopped

25mm (1in) piece ginger (gingerroot), grated

2 tablespoons plain (all-purpose) flour

2 teaspoons ground coriander

2 teaspoons ground cumin

2 teaspoons ground turmeric

1 cup vegetable stock (broth)

1 cup puréed tomatoes (passata)

750g (1½lb) mixed root vegetables, such as potato, sweet potato (yam), celeriac and swede (rutabaga), diced

2 carrots, thinly sliced

freshly ground black pepper

steamed couscous and coriander (cilantro), to serve

1 Heat the oil in a large saucepan. Add the onion, chilli, garlic and ginger (gingerroot) and cook, stirring occasionally, for 3 minutes. Stir in the flour, coriander, cumin and turmeric and cook gently, stirring, for 2 minutes to release the flavours.

2 Transfer mixture to a slow cooker and stir in the stock (broth), then add the puréed tomatoes (passata), diced root vegetables and carrots. Season with pepper and mix well. Cook on high for 3¼ hours or until the vegetables are tender. Serve with steamed couscous and garnish with coriander (cilantro).

Leeks with Beans

Serves 6 · Preparation and cooking 4½–9½ hours

250g (8oz) dried black eyed (navy) beans, soaked overnight

1 tablespoon vegetable oil

1 large onion, chopped

2 cloves garlic, crushed

500g (1lb) leeks, sliced and washed

¼ cup parsley, chopped, plus extra to garnish

6 tomatoes, peeled, deseeded and chopped

1 tablespoon raw sugar

1 teaspoon mustard powder

2 bay leaves

½ teaspoon dried marjoram

1 tablespoon tomato paste (purée)

¼ cup vegetable stock (broth)

salt and freshly ground black pepper

1 Drain the beans well. Heat the oil in a frying pan (skillet) and sauté the onion and garlic, then add the leeks and sauté until softened. Spoon leek mixture, beans and all remaining ingredients into slow cooker.

2 Cover and cook on low for approximately 8–9 hours or on high for 4–5 hours. Garnish with extra parsley.

Baking and Desserts

Believe it or not, slow cookers are great for bread-making – from proving the dough right through to cooking the loaf. They work well for cakes and desserts, too, as the slow cooking process keeps them deliciously moist.

Herb Bread

Makes 1 loaf · Preparation and cooking 3–4 hours

1 tablespoon compressed yeast or
2 teaspoons dried yeast

1 teaspoon white (granulated) sugar

500g (1lb) plain (all-purpose) flour

1 teaspoon vegetable or garlic salt

2 teaspoons dried mixed herbs

2 teaspoons dried chives, crumbled

2 sprigs parsley, chopped

30g (1oz) butter

1 Crumble the yeast into a bowl, stir in sugar and 1¼ cups lukewarm water until yeast has dissolved, or follow the instructions on the packet of dried yeast. Sprinkle with a little of the flour and stand in a warm spot until mixture froths.

2 Mix together flour, salt and herbs. Rub in the butter, then make a well in the centre of the dry ingredients and pour in frothy yeast mixture. Stir well with a wooden spoon, then turn out onto a floured board and knead for about 5 minutes. Shape into a round, place back into bowl and set aside on a slow cooker set on low until dough has doubled in size.

3 Punch down risen dough and form into a round. Place in a greased 22cm (8½in) springform cake tin and set aside on the slow cooker again until dough has doubled in size.

4 Cover tin, place in the slow cooker and cook on high for 2–3 hours, taking care not to remove either the cooker or the cake tin lid until the last hour of cooking time. Turn loaf out and allow to cool on a wire rack. Serve dusted with a little extra flour.

Half and Half Loaf

Makes 2 loaves · Preparation and cooking 3½ hours

2 tablespoons compressed yeast or
4 teaspoons dried yeast

2 teaspoons treacle (molasses) or honey

2⅓ cups warm milk

500g (1lb) plain (all-purpose) flour

500g (1lb) wholemeal (whole wheat) flour

1 tablespoon baking powder

1 tablespoon salt

60g (2oz) butter

6 tablespoons sesame seeds

1 egg white

1　Blend together yeast and treacle (molasses) or honey, then add the milk. Sprinkle a little of the flour on top of the liquid. Stand bowl in a warm spot until mixture froths.

2　Mix together the flours, baking powder and salt. Rub in the butter. Make a well in centre of the dry ingredients and pour in the frothy yeast mixture. Stir well with a wooden spoon, then turn out onto a floured board and knead for about 5 minutes. Shape into a round, place back into bowl and set aside on a slow cooker set on low until dough has doubled in size.

3　Grease two 500g (1lb) bread tins and sprinkle half the sesame seeds around base and sides of tin. Punch down risen dough and form into two rough loaves, then place in tins. Set aside on the slow cooker again until dough has risen to the top of the tins.

4　Preheat the oven to 200°C (180°C fan, 400°F, gas 6). Brush risen loaves with egg white and sprinkle with sesame seeds, then place into oven on middle shelf. Bake for 10 minutes, then reduce temperature to 180°C (160°C fan, 350°F, gas 4) and bake for a further 40–45 minutes. Turn loaves out of tins and allow to cool on a wire rack.

Yoghurt Banana Bread

Makes 1 loaf · Preparation and cooking 3 hours 40 minutes

60g (2oz) butter

120g (4oz) caster (berry) sugar

1 egg, lightly beaten

2 large bananas, pulped

250g (8oz) self-raising wholemeal (whole wheat) flour

pinch of salt

120g (4oz) walnuts, roughly chopped

3 tablespoons natural yoghurt

cinnamon and icing (confectioner's) sugar, to finish

1 Cream together the butter and caster (berry) sugar. Add egg and banana pulp and mix thoroughly.

2 Mix flour and salt together and add walnuts. Add flour mixture and yoghurt alternately to the banana mixture in small quantities and blend thoroughly.

3 Grease a 12 x 22cm (4½ x 8½in) loaf tin, spoon in mixture and cover with lid. Place in slow cooker and cook on high for approximately 2½–3 hours or until a skewer inserted in the banana bread comes out clean. Allow to cool for 10 minutes then turn out onto a wire rack to cool fully.

4 Sprinkle with mixed cinnamon and icing (confectioner's) sugar and serve sliced and spread with butter.

Rich Berry Dessert Cake

Serves 8 · Preparation and cooking 3½ hours

120g (4oz) butter

¼ cup caster (berry) sugar

1½ teaspoons vanilla extract

2 eggs, lightly beaten

2 cups plain (all-purpose) flour

2 teaspoons baking powder

salt

1 teaspoon mixed spice

½ cup milk

¾ cup berries of your choice

cinnamon and icing (confectioner's) sugar, to finish

thickened (whipping) cream, to serve

1   Cream the butter, caster (berry) sugar and vanilla, then fold eggs into mixture.

2   Sift flour, baking powder and salt together and stir in mixed spice. Add spiced flour and milk alternately to the butter mixture, folding in gently and commencing and concluding with the flour. Spoon into a greased and floured 20cm (8in) springform cake tin, smooth the surface and arrange berries on top.

3   Cover and place in slow cooker. Cook on high for approximately 3 hours, taking care not to remove either the cooker or the cake tin lid until the last hour of cooking. Sprinkle with cinnamon and icing (confectioner's) sugar and serve hot or cold, with thickened (whipping) cream.

Cherry and Walnut Fruit Cake

Makes 1 cake · Preparation and cooking 5–5½ hours

250g (8oz) butter

250g (8oz) brown sugar

5 eggs, beaten to a froth

500g (1lb) sultanas (golden raisins)

170g (6oz) glacé (glazed) cherries

120g (4oz) walnut pieces

200g (7oz) plain (all-purpose) flour

1 tablespoon milk

1 Cream the butter and sugar in a bowl. Add eggs gradually. Fold in fruit, walnuts and flour, then add milk.

2 Grease a 22cm (8½in) springform cake tin and line its sides and base with baking paper. Spoon in the cake mixture, cover and place in slow cooker. Cook on high for 4½–5 hours, taking care not to remove either the cooker or the cake tin lid until the last hour of cooking.

Caramel Rice and Apricot Pudding

Serves 6 · Preparation and cooking 1¾–6¼ hours

1 cup evaporated milk

1 teaspoon vanilla extract

⅔ cup soft brown sugar

2½ cups rice, cooked but still slightly firm

60g (2oz) butter, melted

½ teaspoon mixed spice

½ cup canned apricots, drained

1 Beat together evaporated milk, vanilla and sugar. Combine with remaining ingredients, pour mixture into a greased ovenproof dish and cover with foil.

2 Place dish in slow cooker and cook on high for 1½–2 hours or on low for 4–6 hours. Stir occasionally during the first 30 minutes or so of cooking.

Orange-wheel Steamed Pudding

Serves 6–8 · Preparation and cooking 5½ hours

2 oranges, peeled and thickly sliced, plus zest of 1 orange

90g (3oz) butter

½ cup raw sugar

1½ cups self-raising flour

salt

½ cup milk

1 egg, beaten

2 tablespoons golden (corn) syrup or honey, plus extra to serve

cream, to serve

1 Grease a medium-sized pudding basin and arrange orange slices around the base and sides.

2 Cream together butter and sugar until light and fluffy. Stir in flour and salt to taste alternately with milk and egg, then beat until smooth. Stir in grated orange zest.

3 Warm golden (corn) syrup or honey and spoon over the base and sides of the orange-lined basin. Spoon in pudding mixture, cover basin tightly with foil and tie with string, forming a loop at the top so that the basin may be easily removed from the slow cooker.

4 Place basin in slow cooker. Boil 2–4 cups water and pour into base of cooker, then cook on high for approximately 5 hours. Carefully remove the pudding basin and turn pudding out. Slice the pudding and serve with a little extra warmed golden syrup or honey spooned over each slice, topped with a dab of cream.

Baked Bread and Butter Pudding

Serves 6 · Preparation and cooking 3¾–4¾ hours

4 thin slices stale brown or white bread, buttered

½ cup mixed sultanas (golden raisins) and currants

3 tablespoons raw sugar

½ teaspoon grated nutmeg (mace) or cinnamon

2 eggs

2½ cups milk

1 teaspoon vanilla extract

zest of ½ orange, grated

1   Remove crusts from bread and cut into thick fingers. Grease an ovenproof dish and arrange bread in layers, buttered-side up. Sprinkle layers with dried fruit, sugar and spice.

2   Beat together eggs, milk and vanilla and stir in orange zest. Pour mixture over layered bread and allow to stand for approximately 30 minutes. Cover dish with lid or foil.

3   Pour 1 cup hot water into the slow cooker, then insert the pudding dish and cook on high for 3–4 hours.

Weights and Measures

Weights and measures differ from country to country, but with these handy conversion charts cooking has never been easier!

Cup Measurements

One cup of these commonly used ingredients is equal to the following weights.

Ingredient	Metric	Imperial
Apples (dried and chopped)	125g	4½oz
Apricots (dried and chopped)	190g	6¾oz
Breadcrumbs (packet)	125g	4½oz
Breadcrumbs (soft)	55g	2oz
Butter	225g	8oz
Cheese (shredded/grated)	115g	4oz
Choc bits	155g	5½oz
Coconut (desiccated/fine)	90g	3oz
Flour (plain/all-purpose, self-raising)	115g	4oz
Fruit (dried)	170g	6oz
Golden (corn) syrup	315g	11oz
Honey	315g	11oz
Margarine	225g	8oz
Nuts (chopped)	115g	4oz
Rice (cooked)	155g	5½oz
Rice (uncooked)	225g	8oz
Sugar (brown)	155g	5½oz
Sugar (caster/berry/superfine)	225g	8oz
Sugar (granulated)	225g	8oz
Sugar (sifted, icing/confectioner's)	155g	5½oz
Treacle (molasses)	315g	11oz

Oven Temperatures

Celsius	Fahrenheit	Gas mark
120	250	1
150	300	2
160	320	3
180	350	4
190	375	5
200	400	6
220	430	7
230	450	8
250	480	9

Weight Measures

Metric	Imperial
10g	¼oz
15g	½oz
20g	¾oz
30g	1oz
60g	2oz
115g	4oz (¼lb)
125g	4½oz
145g	5oz
170g	6oz
185g	6½oz
200g	7oz
225g	8oz (½lb)
300g	10½oz
330g	11½oz
370g	13oz
400g	14oz
425g	15oz
455g	16oz (1lb)
500g	17½oz (1lb 1½oz)
600g	21oz (1lb 5oz)
650g	23oz (1lb 7oz)
750g	26½oz (1lb 10½oz)
1000g (1kg)	35oz (2lb 3oz)

Liquid Measures

Cup	Metric	Imperial
¼ cup	63ml	2¼fl oz
½ cup	125ml	4½fl oz
¾ cup	188ml	6⅔fl oz
1 cup	250ml	8¾fl oz
1¾ cup	438ml	15½fl oz
2 cups	500ml	17½fl oz
4 cups	1 litre	35fl oz

Spoon	Metric	Imperial
¼ teaspoon	1.25ml	1/25fl oz
½ teaspoon	2.5ml	1/12fl oz
1 teaspoon	5ml	⅙fl oz
1 tablespoon	15ml	½fl oz

Index